BEYONCÉ

★ POP STAR ★

KATIE LAJINESS

Big Buddy Books
An Imprint of Abdo Publishing
abdopublishing.com

BIG
BUDDY POP BIOGRAPHIES

abdopublishing.com

Published by Abdo Publishing, a division of ABDO, PO Box 398166, Minneapolis, Minnesota 55439.
Copyright © 2018 by Abdo Consulting Group, Inc. International copyrights reserved in all countries.
No part of this book may be reproduced in any form without written permission from the publisher.
Big Buddy Books™ is a trademark and logo of Abdo Publishing.

Printed in the United States of America, North Mankato, Minnesota.
052017
092017

THIS BOOK CONTAINS
RECYCLED MATERIALS

Cover Photo: WENN Ltd/Alamy Stock Photo.
Interior Photos: ASSOCIATED PRESS (pp. 9, 11, 15, 19); Chris Pizzello/Invision/AP (pp. 6, 23); fmpg/
     MediaPunch/MediaPunch/Ipx/AP (p. 27); Frank Micelotta/Invision/AP (p. 9); Invision for
     Parkwood Entertainment/AP (p. 25); ITAR-TASS Photo Agency/Alamy Stock Photo (p. 15);
     Jemal Countess/Staff/Getty (p. 17); Matt Sayles/Invision/AP (p. 29); REUTERS/Alamy Stock
     Photo (p. 13); United Archives GmbH/Alamy Stock Photo (p. 21); WENN Ltd/Alamy Stock
     Photo (p. 5).

Coordinating Series Editor: Tamara L. Britton
Graphic Design: Jenny Christensen

Publisher's Cataloging-in-Publication Data

Names: Lajiness, Katie, author.
Title: Beyoncé / by Katie Lajiness.
Description: Minneapolis, MN : Abdo Publishing, 2018. | Series: Big buddy
     pop biographies | Includes bibliographical references and index.
Identifiers: LCCN 2016962358 | ISBN 9781532110580 (lib. bdg.) |
     ISBN 9781680788433 (ebook)
Subjects: LCSH: Beyoncé, 1981- --Juvenile literature. | Rhythm and blues
     musician--United States--Biography--Juvenile literature. | Singers--United
     States--Biography--Juvenile literature.
Classification: DDC 782.42164092 [B]--dc23
LC record available at http://lccn.loc.gov/2016962358

CONTENTS

QUEEN BEY

Beyoncé Knowles is a famous **entertainer**. She has recorded **award**-winning albums. And, she has traveled to different countries on her world tours. Beyoncé is also an actress. She has appeared on TV shows and in many movies.

SNAPSHOT

NAME:
Beyoncé Giselle Knowles

BIRTHDAY:
September 4, 1981

BIRTHPLACE:
Houston, Texas

POPULAR ALBUMS:
4, Beyoncé, Lemonade

FAMILY TIES

Beyoncé Giselle Knowles was born in Houston, Texas, on September 4, 1981. Her parents are Mathew and Tina Knowles. Beyoncé has a younger sister named Solange.

Beyoncé's sister is also a singer. In 2017, Solange won her first Grammy Award.

WHERE IN THE WORLD?

Oklahoma

Arkansas

New Mexico

Texas

Louisiana

Houston

MEXICO

GULF OF MEXICO

N
W E
S

EARLY YEARS

As a young girl, Beyoncé was a natural **performer**. She grew up singing at church. When Beyoncé was seven, she won the first of many talent **competitions**. People soon noticed her gift for singing and dancing.

DID YOU KNOW?
Growing up, Beyoncé won more than 30 talent shows.

As a child, Beyoncé took dance lessons. Today, she is known for her dance moves.

GIRL GROUPS

When Beyoncé was nine, she joined a **hip-hop** group called Girls Tyme. In 1993, the group appeared on a TV talent show called *Star Search*. Girls Tyme won second place!

In 1997, Beyoncé formed another group called Destiny's Child. They became one of the best-selling girl groups of all time. Then, in 2005, Destiny's Child decided to take a break.

In 2001, Destiny's Child won two Grammy Awards for their song "Say My Name."

Destiny's Child joined Beyoncé for a performance during the 2013 Super Bowl Halftime Show.

11

GOING SOLO

While still with Destiny's Child, Beyoncé decided to make her own music. In 2003, she **released** her first **solo** album.

Beyoncé went on tour across western Europe to **promote** *Dangerously in Love*. In 2004, she won five **Grammy Awards** for this album.

DID YOU KNOW?
Destiny's Child broke up in 2005.

Fans loved *Dangerously in Love*. It sold 4 million copies in the United States.

Beyoncé was on her way to becoming a great **pop** star. In 2006, she **released** *B'Day*. It included hit songs "Irreplaceable" and "Beautiful Liar." The album reached number one on the Billboard 200 chart.

Her next album, *I Am … Sasha Fierce* came out in 2008. This album included two discs. The *I Am* disc featured slow songs. And, the *Sasha Fierce* disc was all pop music.

In 2005, Beyoncé performed with singer Josh Groban at the Academy Awards. They sang "Believe" from *The Polar Express* soundtrack.

During her *I Am* music tour, Beyoncé had an all-female band.

SINGING STAR

Beyoncé was becoming one of the biggest **celebrities** in the world. In 2010, she and Lady Gaga **released** "Telephone." The song was on the Billboard Hot 100 chart for 33 weeks.

In 2011, Beyoncé was the top act at England's Glastonbury Festival. A few days later, her fourth album came out. She called it 4. The album's top song was "Best Thing I Never Had."

Beyoncé and Lady Gaga (*left*) are friends who support each other. In 2009, they went to a Women in Music event together.

In 2013, Beyoncé was invited to sing at President Barack Obama's **inauguration**. This was a special honor.

Later that year, her self-titled album *Beyoncé* came out. This visual album included 17 music videos. In its first three days, more than 800,000 copies were sold.

Beyoncé's sixth **solo** album, *Lemonade*, was **released** in 2016. She made history with this album. All 12 songs made the Billboard Hot 100 chart at the same time.

Beyoncé sang "The Star-Spangled Banner" at President Obama's inauguration.

SCREEN TIME

Beyoncé is also an actress. In 2001, she starred in the MTV movie, *Carmen: A Hip Hopera*. She's been in movies such as *The Pink Panther* and *The Fighting Temptations*. In *Dreamgirls* and *Cadillac Records*, Beyoncé plays a singer.

Beyoncé starred in *The Pink Panther* with actors Steve Martin (*center*) and Jean Reno (*left*).

AWARDS

Fans love to see Beyoncé at **award** shows. As of 2017, she has been **nominated** for 62 **Grammy Awards**. This is more nominations than any other female **pop** artist. She has won 22 of the awards.

DID YOU KNOW ?

In 2016, Minnesota Governor Mark Dayton made May 23 Beyoncé Day.

In 2017, Beyoncé won Grammy Awards for Best Music Video and Best Urban Contemporary Album.

23

GIVING BACK

Giving to **charity** is important to Beyoncé. During her 2016 Formation world tour, part of her ticket sales went to three charities.

Beyoncé also helps sick children. In Singapore, Beyoncé visited a hospital. There, she sang her hit song "Halo" to sick children. During a concert, Beyoncé once brought a sick child on stage and sang "Survivor."

In 2016, *Forbes* magazine ranked Beyoncé as number 18 on its list of the World's 100 Most Powerful Women.

25

OFF THE STAGE

Offstage, Beyoncé leads a private life with her family. In 2008, she married **rapper** Jay Z. In 2012, they welcomed a daughter named Blue Ivy.

Beyoncé is also a successful businesswoman. She has a clothing line, a food company, and her own record label.

DID YOU KNOW?
In 2017, Beyoncé and Jay Z announced they are expecting twins.

Jay Z and Blue Ivy joined Beyoncé at the 2014 MTV Video Music Awards.

BUZZ

Today, Beyoncé is one of the world's biggest **celebrities**. She continues to charm and surprise her fans. Everyone is excited to see what Beyoncé does next!

At the 2017 Grammy Awards, Beyoncé sang "Love Drought" and "Sandcastles."

GLOSSARY

award something that is given in recognition of good work or a good act.

celebrity a famous or celebrated person.

charity a group or a fund that helps people in need.

competition (kahm-puh-TIH-shuhn) a contest between two or more persons or groups.

entertainer a person who performs for public entertainment.

Grammy Award any of the awards given each year by the National Academy of Recording Arts and Sciences. Grammy Awards honor the year's best accomplishments in music.

hip-hop a form of popular music that features rhyme, spoken words, and electronic sounds. It is similar to rap music.

inauguration (ih-naw-gyuh-RAY-shuhn) a ceremony in which a person is sworn into office.

nominate to name as a possible winner.

perform to do something in front of an audience. A performer is someone who performs. A performance is the act of doing something, such as singing or acting, in front of an audience.

pop relating to popular music.

promote to help something become known.

rapper someone who raps. To rap is to speak the words of a song to a beat.

release to make available to the public.

solo a performance by a single person.

WEBSITES

To learn more about Pop Biographies, visit **abdobooklinks.com**. These links are routinely monitored and updated to provide the most current information available.

INDEX